My

Beautiful

Alone

by Stormy Chalmers

My Beautiful Alone

Published by:
Southeast Media
87 Piedmont Drive
Palm Coast, Florida 32164
USA
Phone (386) 206-1163

Jess' Sandcastle

Build a sandcastle for me
by the shore
With lots of towers and
seashell doors

With windows made
of coral reef
and its own little
beach

Build me a sandcaslte
all my own
for my dreams
to call home

Split

*You're different by
day than you are
by night*

*timid, weak and
unwilling to fight*

*then night comes
and you change*

*daring then crazy
like your soul
rearranges*

*are you the same
person or do you
have two people inside*

*Does one hide by
day and the
other by night?*

Don't understand
how this could be
but I think I love
you both equally

A kiss to bring you
comfort while I'm away
and to remember me by
at the end of each day

I am...

Who am I you want to know
am I friend or am I foe
Who am I you wish ask
take a peek if you're up to the task

Irresistible pain
killer of my dreams
Give me what I wanted
just to take it away

Irresistible poison
all you bring is pain
wanted to be invisible
Now you know my name

Irresistible poison
I'd drink you every time
No matter the consequence
Just to claim you mine.

M'lady's Heart

And in vain M'lady
tries to save her
hero from destruction

They've gathered
up into a lake
for her lover's
dead

Her heart's as
cold as stone
Soul's gone to
heaven

And M'lady will
love no other

to a dead hero

her heart was
given.

Flowers

A tulip for my hopeless love
a lily for purity
an Iris for the message
and a rose to show I love thee

Just for you...

I gave to you my heart a long time ago
You dropped it and laughed when it broke
I picked up the fallen parts and
glued them back together
I handed you my innocent white wings
you snapped them before threw them back at
me
I cried unable to tape the pieces straight
you snickered when I mentioned fate
Now I give you my eternal soul to
Put in a jam jar with all my dreams and
hopes
Encase my body under the ground
And write my name in stone
You'll remember what I gave to you
when you're left all alone

And if I go to hell I hope you'll meet me there
Because I'll always love you,
even if you never care.

Dreaming...

The rain falls softly in the background of my dreams never closer, but never farther away. It disappears before it hits the ground making a soft mist that swirls almost unseen around my feet. I can hear the sweet sound of a harp floating about me, barely there, from a place beyond the reach of my eyes. I can feel the wind ruffle through my hair and the waters lapping at the hem of my skirt as if it was beckoning for me to journey into its depths, telling me to stay and never leave. I wish that this was truly able to be: to stay wrapped up safe in the waves, disappearing into the ocean and becoming one with the sea-foam. Never having to visit the world above. Alas, it is but a dream and as the shores of sleep recede, the dawn comes quickly to keep me, steal me away. As I try to grasp a wisp of my dream, to bring it with me to the waking world, I find that it slips through my fingers like the wind, wishing to be free. Then Dawn drags me kicking and screaming into the light of morning without remorse. For I fear that if it didn't, I would stay here forever and live under the sea with only the kelp to keep me as a companion. Otherwise I would stay there alone to dream of the world I left behind.

Home

This prison I call home
nothing to call my own
this manner that I live
I give everything
but nothing do I get
I suffer the torment
suffer the pain
waiting for some one
to take me away

Strong Men

Some say only weak men
cry tears, but I must disagree
for only strong men let their
tears flow free
The brave for loved ones
people long dead
And for sad stories they've
just read
I say that strong men cry

Life

*Once standing
in a crowded room
feeling so alone
But no one even knew*

*Sometimes I wonder
what is wrong with me
why I put on a happy mask
so people can't see me*

*It hurts sometimes
that no one knows
what I feel inside and
what is on my mind*

*When I lay awake at night
Whispers in my ears
I dream of angels
telling me not to fear*

Sometimes life is scary
a place full of fears
I might scream out loud
Would you hear?

+*Hidden*+

Passed over
left behind
No one looks
when I cry

Looked over
hid away
No one loves me
they stay away

Left alone
gone for good
no one even
understood

I am hidden away

Hidden away in plain view
Hoping that no one will see you
Carried away wanting to see
Wondering about your enemies
Loving to learn and learning to love
Pondering how it is done
Wishing and hoping longing to see
Thinking of how this could be

Enchanted

My enchanted enemy
how does your realm fare?
Perhaps I will see it
when I meet you there

My enchanted enemy
the hope the future holds
What you do seems to always
come back tenfold

My enchanted enemy
come you from shores deep
and when you come to the surface
for you the sky shall weep

My enchanted enemy
will you mind what I've said
Hopefully one day I shall
meet with you again

Blank pages fill my mind
this is how I pass the time
To put my thoughts on paper
the words flow through my pen
today the sky was blue
Tomorrow will it be again

Express Yourself

emotions are hard to express
do it wrong your life's a mess

Some people get hurt, some even cry
It all happens when you let emotions fly

If you get mad don't have a cow
If you're happy please don't frown

Bend in ways you
never knew you could
compromise when you wouldn't
have before
It's a shock to your system
can't get enough
Sometimes it's harder when it's easy
than when it's tough

I've twisted my thinking cap on
plugged myself in
I'd like to tell you all about it
But the words are jumbled in my pen
the background fades to match my skin
I never wanted to blend in
Fate didn't mean it
And it was just a wake up call
Hope they didn't set you up
Just to make you fall
Spill the stars across the sky
Just don't pause to say goodbye
Wish I could just fly away
To be with you another day

Lost

I keep the real me locked away
hidden
where? I can't say
No need for friends
though I long for talk
I wonder when my heart when dark
I've tried to find myself
but can't you see
A long the way I've both the map
and the key
I've given up now there is no hope
For I can't remember the words I just wrote

Inspiration

The whiteness of the blank pages stares at me ...
Telling me to start.
So ...
I'm looking for it,
my inspiration.

Have you found it?

Can you lead me there?

Inspire me,
Show me how it feels.

They wished for me to fill it,
the ghost white of the page.

I couldn't before but now I can.

I've found my inspiration,
it was always here.

You inspire me.

Told

You told me
I hated you and
I believed you

You told me
I loved you
I believed you then too

You told me that
maybe, just maybe
you loved me back

I believed you
just because I
Like to make you mad

*You told me
to say goodbye
and I did*

And you won

*You told me that
you wouldn't hurt me
I believed you*

I shouldn't have, huh?

My heart's paper cut

*Rip my heart out.
Take it.
Lock it up,
Or throw it all away.
doesn't matter my scars will still remain.*

Can't you see them?
Right here or there?
No.

Well you wouldn't would you ...

Even if you put them there

Rip out my heart.
Lock in a box . . .
I'll wait for you to leave
before I pick the lock.

Wish

Invisibility is what some wish
When others wish simply to be seen

Neither needs the other

but want with all their hearts

You don't need to see it
for it to fall apart

Livin' in the Suburbs

Nobody knows what I'm really like
Living in the suburbs, having a normal life
But when the sun does down you better watch out
Because when night fall comes my wild side
comes out
The lights flash the music blares and all around
me people stare
They come and ask me where I've been all this
time
They laugh when I tell them, Living in the suburbs
living a normal life

. . . Ghost town . . .

Welcome to my ghost town
where my memories live
thought it would last forever
but it didn't in the end

Welcome to my ghost town
here we let sleeping dogs lie
don't fix it if it's working
to tell the truth or just truthful lies

Welcome to my ghost town
my never ending loop
remember when you went away
and left us without hope

Welcome to my ghost town

27

hope you enjoyed your stay
but will you catch my kiss
before you fade away

Standing

I used to stand here
all alone
This place I once
called home
I used to be real
but now I'm not
now just a silent shadow
stands in my spot

Embrace

Do what no one else can seem to
fully embrace the wind
Turn your face to the sky
and catch a glimpse of heaven
Trick the devil and
save your soul
Question the answers you
were told
Give in and embrace
the wind
Where you start
affects where you end

What I Knew

I'm lost in my sea of sorrow
unsure of where to turn

All around me lays the water
and the shore is far away

I never thought you'd leave me here
But I knew you'd never stay

The darkness holds
me in its arms
as if to keep
me from harm

I wraps around
me like a cloak
so tightly I feel
like I could choke

It covers my
heart and I
feel like I was
ripped apart

The dark has stolen
part of my soul
now I never shall
be whole

Painting

want to paint a picture
no words could describe
to show you how beautiful
you are in my eyes

want to keep you
all for myself
make you understand
you're like no one else

And I want to show you
my soul because
without you I'd never be whole

Beyond Perfect

Perfect in chaos
a path without an end
love unrequited
wishing to be pretend

Memories of amnesia
a heart without a soul
answers but not questions
for lies yet told

Nightmares made of dreams
innocents bathed in blood
path of least redemption
hell from above

Forever ago

Twisting
Turning
Hoping
Yearning
trying to escape
this dreary black hole
Loving
Learning
Stomach churning
can't find relief
just want to go home

+*Get HIGH*+

You look like a potato feels
but alas do I taste like a
tomato smells?
Lions are pretty
as only lions are
Not pretty which is
beautiful yet not
so much as ugly which
wouldn't be pretty at all
Oh, to be a biscuit !
And have hair that
feels like thick life
To have someone as
a friend because their
name is theirs
Swallow buttons just
for fun because if you

lean over far enough
your eyeballs might fall out

Would you?

Would you still love me if I took the coward's way
or would you want me to be brave?
You're tears will rip my heart apart
will you finish before you start?

Would you seek safety in my arms
when your friends try to do you harm?
Your endless sorrow causes my soul to ache
you're asleep even when you're awake.

Would you spend forever with me, if I asked you to,
or would you simply just refuse?
Your plate is full with problems of the world.
If I gave my life to you, would you give me yours?

Smile for me

I told you to stop hiding but still you ran away
just stop hiding from me
It won't make your problems go away

Could you die for the greater good
for true love would you fight
Have you tried to save me
Shall you cry for me tonight

Will you die for happiness
for freedom or for love
Will you smile for me
like you smile just for her

To have someone but to not have them whole
Sometimes is worse
then to have no one at all

Freedom from your pain
all I see is your face
Can't be happy without you
Can I find you if you leave this place

Nightmare

It sees you
it stalks you
it follows when you run
It knows where you hide and
where you keep your gun
it can hide in the shadows
or in the brightest daylight
And it doesn't matter where you run
It will find you hiding

Deja Vu

Have I ever met you?
Deja Vu
Have I ever seen you?

You take me
You make me yours
I feel as if I've been here before

Why do I love you?
Deja Vu
Why do I have to?

You hurt me
You make me feel pain
My whole world's gone up in flames

How did this begin?
Deja Vu
How will it end?

You leave me here to die again
I think you always knew
how this would end.

Deja Vu
Have I ever met you?

Cry

A baby cries for her mother
a maid for her lover
We cry for our true loves

A wife cries for her husband
a daughter for a father
We cry for parts of our lost souls

A child cries in hunger
a young girl in fear
We all cry because their cries we hear

A Brother cries in morning
a boy for his sickly dog
We all cry because we know it all

Blind Hearts

Love is blind
and so are you
don't know what you put me through
You think that
you can see
But I know you can't, not really
Love is blind
and so's my heart
Because without you I'd fall apart

To Find

Look in the forest
to find what they took
But run away before they look
Wonder about mysteries
Scandals and lies
Don't worry when rumours start to fly

Turn away from
hurt and pain
Have you realized it's no game

Once was
truth turns false
Hope you realize what you lost

Just

Save my soul, save my heart
save me
before I fall apart

Don't leave me now, Don't say goodbye
I haven't
anymore tears to cry

Go away, go back home
go and
you leave me alone

Help me, help yourself
help everyone
save themselves

Don't worry, don't wonder, Don't even cry

I never
had a chance to say goodbye

Save my soul, save my life
save me
Keep me alive

Finding you

Without you here I can't find
the light
Although everything around
me is bright
Feels like I've fallen from grace
to see you
Would heal my broken wings

We could fly away together far

into the night
And together we could be Dreaming
our whole lives

Falling

My wings have broken
my heart is worn
my eyes hold sorrow
That won't leave in the morn

Your soul is shattered
your mind has split
your voice holds memories
You shan't forget

We won't fly away together

we won't find the key
we will fall as one
Into an endless sea

To think you could save her
You stare into the space she occupies
to hope she notices you
You say that you despise her
But everyone knows you don't
Look after her as she leaves
And wish you could follow
To think you could save her
How young you were then
Now you've made her hate you
For all the tainted love you've shown
She's never really there
When you talk to her
You wish she would love you
The one thing she'll never do

These wings of mine

Grow wings and fly away
What I dream of every day
To leave here and break my chains
Grow wings and fly away

To capture flame and
Lock it in a cage
Save it up to give to you
when me meet again

Hold my tears in my hands
To hope to make you understand
Why my heart shatters this way

Grow wings and fly away
What I dream of every day

I hope for something I can't achieve
Although I know it won't ever be

Tumbling Paradox

To tumble through a looking glass
to see beyond your sight
Leave with me today or
Stay with me tonight

Battle with a queen
who sees in black and red
Turing your face upward
You're looking down instead

Poems that look better backwards
A truth made of lies
A watch fixed with jam and butter
An impossible disguise

Chess games to decide your fate
Sense from insensible things
A maze that's filled with playing cards
Twins decidedly insane

Grinning cats from high in the trees
And a darkened path to follow
Atop a mushroom a fortune teller
From large to small in a bite or swallow

Queen of flowers

The proud Queen of flowers
Her shining crown of lead
Her true love used to call her that
But he never will again

She danced in a dress made of flowers
Her laughter filled with joy
Now her true love's left her
And her true love is no more

She danced one last time
In her flower made dress
Her helpless laughter full of sadness
She wishes to see her true love again . . .

The proud Queen of flowers
Her shining crown of lead
Her true love used to call her that
But he never will again
She danced with the depths
In her flower made dress
With no hero to save her
And a crown made of lead

The proud Queen of flowers
Her shining crown of lead
She's gone to the depths
To see her true love again

When

When the light left me
the darkness held me
and smoothed away my fears

As the light rejected me
the darkness accepted me
and kissed away my tears

When the light beckoned me
to return the darkness
warned me away from them

The light asked why
I didn't lie
And I told them the truth

When you rejected me
The darkness kept me
because they care more than you

Simple Story

A tune forgotten long ago
A story that's now lost
It's about a boy and the war
that he fought

He was Just a young lad
not past fourteen
such a sad story
for a boy, barley a teen

He stole away on
a ship headed for the fight
When he got off it
was far into the night

He then saw a land full of fear

men leaning over others
their eyes full of tears

There where men caring others
people long dead
Some with no arms
Some with no heads

He was stricken and had to look away
He hadn't been there even a day

Still the boy walked
Bravely into the camp
No one even gave him a
passing glance

They issued him some gear
and gave him a tent
Tomorrow he was to
fight with the men

The morning came early
it came with the light
They told the boy

Today you must fight

The boy nodded his head
and bravely walked out
when he heard a shattered
scream and then a shout

The men took off running
the boy in the lead
A shot was fired and the
fighting began
that day the boy was made into a man

the men woke at the
battle's sound
They rushed to stop the
enemy's course

An arrow was fired
and in the boy's heart found it's mark
the boy was afraid as he
screamed and fell down

None but one soldier heard his cry

and to him the boy said a fearful goodbye
the man leaned and took the boy's hand
That day the boy had become a man

He fought for his country
as he fought for his life
the solider held that man as he let
go of life

A tune that's remembered
and A story's been found
Seems my heart is broken
For my love's in the ground

Facade

try to stand up to your
stance of perfection
but I'm never good enough

struggle to meet your
strictest measure
but it's like I'm just to short

Holding up this facade
just as I'm expected

And as always I'll never
be just perfect enough for you
Because this as close as I'll ever be

Falter

I thought you were full of fire
full of heart and of soul
But then I realized that you falter
at the moment you should have stood tall

I thought you and I where two
halves of a whole
But you're different than I'll
ever know

This story's too picturesque for there
not to be a flaw
I know what it is now . . .
You falter when I need you the most

+butterflies+

Speak to language of the sea
and seek forgotten starlight
watch roses drown in
puddles of your tears
just speak up when
you tight to fear
love is only found in fairy tales
as we're all to blame
All you want is to see
the daylight
But the shadows
won't let you flee
Now give your dreams
to butterflies to soar away
to heaven

Silent winds carry softly away the petals
of cherry blossoms bloomed at midnight
They use your tears for water
Your smile instead of sunlight
Remember when you knew the devil
and his heart that you still hold
Walk guilty in the moonlight
a body without a heart and without a soul

Flowers

Single flower to stand alone
as our walls come tumbling down
in the rubble the sun shines
and a single ray of hope is seen

Single flower grow roots strong
Forgive those whom do you wrong
The fires you where sheltered from
consumed your brothers all but one

Single flower you now give life
to other flowers, that stand by your side
but remember when you stood alone
and how you helped to save our home

SEEK

Think of all the things you've done
were you happy, was it fun?
Wonder about all you've been through
would I have done that If I was you?
Speak of things before your time
was it a pinch of ginger or a dash of thyme?
Remember what your mother said
when she tucked you into bed:
Beware of the Christian's devil and it's hell
I don't know if it's true only time will tell.
Think of your future, for you're older now
Seek the answer and the truth
Seems the young always waste their youth

-Forest-

Come with me in the forest deep
as the moon watches over us
come and dance with the fairies there
and leave with the sun to hurry us

Faun prints cover the clearing's grass
as the sun rests in the treetops
the fairies bid us a fond farewell
and you wish that father time would free us

———————————

give me the world on a platter
and I'll give it back to you
Baby, just surrender
and it'll be over soon
give me your heart wrapped in a bow
and I'll give you my soul in a ribbon
your "friends" won't let you forget the past
but Baby, I do and with me you're forgiven
give me wings to fly away
and I'll take you in my arms
Baby, if every star fell from heaven
I'd make sure you were safe from harm
give me the world on a platter
and I'll give it back to you
Because, Baby I don't need the world . . .

All I need is you.

Hating to Love

Hate the person I pretend to be
Because I hate the real me
you know how I'm really fake
and that I hide behind the front I make
Hate you for hating me
wish we were the way we used to be
I dally with 'important' things
you think it's more than just a game
It's like I've wiped away all the years we
spent
and forgotten all the pain
The rest of the world won't affect us
you say and I wonder what if
I want to hate you for hating me
but I can't seem to really mean it
I love you all the time, eight days a week

and even if you never know,
I'll still love you forever and always

The World's Weight

In the Forest a fairy sits
crying softly in the mist
hidden under a mushroom top
no one realizes that she's gone

Under the sea a mermaid swims
in the kelp weeping for her sins
sleeping on an endless reef
her heart's been over filled with grief

An angel child stands on a clouds
forever smiling but waning to frown
the rain is like heaven's tears
an angel child is sobbing but no one hears

Laying quietly a human sleeps
and silent tears run down her cheeks

she's dreaming of an angel, a mermaid and a fairy
And the weight of the world is theirs to carry

Blink

of false hopes and empathy
kill me slowly blatantly
I might seem soulless
until the pain sinks in
human emotions are
truly frail strings
a silent tear falls
and you wonder why
your soul's been shattered
in the blink of an eye
your passion, your fierce fear
seems to fall away
made you cold and unfeeling
with a lying front

in the rain, in the moonlight
I'll sleep the pain away

FOREVER LASTS

Push me closer to the edge
and pull me back again
you were once my enemy
and now you are my friend
Seems I'm no longer moving
towards you but closer to the end
Eternity to go on forever but
I don't think it lasted all that long
Sometimes you have to end
to begin again

Apathy

I was an angel
before you clipped my wings
I gave them to you
and you threw them away

Apathy comes with a price
or so it would seem
You don't even care that
I gave you my whole, my everything

Lucky

Water falling outside the window
to see when I wake up
Rabbit's paw to hang above
my bed for a little luck
Spend the morning picking clovers
to make wishes on
Shake hands with me
and some luck might rub off

You're like a vine of ivy
wrapping around my soul
I keep cutting you down but
you still seem to grow

You're like the evening tide
always pulling me out
when I think I'm swimming in
I'm really swimming out

If lovers liked as they loved
the lovers would love more
with shadows in his heart your lover fears
the dark
Lover's love is forgotten
as lovers love no more
because the lovers have kissed the shadow
and the darkness ate them whole

Inspired

Against all odds we came through
you didn't think I was kidding did you
you didn't believe until death do we part
truth is it kills you when we're apart
What are the odds I've asked
And are you truly up to the task
When we nodded our heads they looked up
in awe
Not many can say they've gotten this far

My Knight

My fugitive prince
You're always with me
never by my side
You always seem second best
Although I know you're better than the rest
you hide in others' shadows
and it keeps you from the light

Dream

Radical dreamer
Dream something for me
My radical dreamer
Please don't forget me
Belong to me no more
Radical dreamer
Just leave me be
Alone in all my misery
My radical dreamer
So that I can dream of you

Melt

I want to melt when you look into my eyes
don't act like you're not surprised
My knees get weak when you whisper my name
This feeling you five me drives me insane
Inside my stomach butterflies roam
When I'm in your arms I'm right at home
You're always laughing to you the world's a joke
Laugh so hard you almost choke
Perhaps I imagined that glazed look in your eyes
I can't stop melting and I'm not surprised

Perfect

I try to stand up to your
Stance of perfection
But I'm never good enough
I struggle to meet your
strictest measure
But it's like I'm just to short
Holding on to this facade
As I'm expected to
And like always I'll never be
Perfect enough for you

Just Me

emotion wiped away
just like unfortunate mistakes
replaced by false impressions
that anyone can see
make me just a little frigid
as I try to find my tattered soul
just lean back on your heels
so the world can pass you by
your face is successfully neutral
and you're wishing to strike out
All you really want to be
is to be just like me

Wonder

Value's been broken
Trust you betrayed
Mock me with silence
As you struggle to breathe

place everything into context
in this spinning mirrored hall
I'll bring you down with me
if you ry to make me fall

Reduce me into shambles
Fill me full of pain
Don't shatter my soul
With the shards don't play

Anything for you, my love

Naive though I promised
I'd sell my soul to the devil
So that you could go to heaven

Once

For every moment that passes
at least one wish is made
some may come true
when others fade away

For everyone knows the prince
is gone forever and that
Snow White may never wake up
when some hold hope
others just give up

About the Author

Stormy Chalmers wrote this book while attending high school in a small Florida town. She spent much of her time at the local library. Her interests included (and still include) drawing, writing and library science.

www.ingramcontent.com/pod-product-compliance
Lightning Source LLC
Chambersburg PA
CBHW061155040426
42445CB00013B/1690